Carving
Santa
Ornaments
with
TOM WOLFE

Schiffer Publishing Ltd

77 Lower Valley Road, Atglen, PA 19310

Copyright 1994 by Tom Wolfe
Library of Congress Number: 94-66378

Printed in China
ISBN: 0-88740-617-3

Published by Schiffer Publishing Ltd.
77 Lower Valley Road
Atglen, PA 19310
Please write for a free catalog.
This book may be purchased from the publisher.
Please include $2.95 postage.
Try your bookstore first.

Contents

Íntroduction

It would be hard to say when the first ornament was used on a tree to celebrate Christmas. We do know that since the customs of Christmas and Santa Claus were popularized in the United States in the nineteenth century, the tree and its decorations have been the center of almost every household at the holiday season.

Styles and fads have shaped the type of decorations that have adorned our trees. We have seen bubble lights and fancy baubles. Ornaments have been made in all shapes and using all sorts of material, from cookie dough to cardboard to fine Italian blown glass and, yes, to wood. Through it all the figure of Santa Claus has been a constant presence in our homes.

In this book I've tried to give you a basic Santa Claus ornament that can be developed and changed as you wish to give a great variety of results. Among the most popular with my customers has been the Banana Santa which you can see in the gallery. The technique lends itself to "saintly" Santas, several of which are also in the gallery.

I've carved the figure large, using 4" basswood, but you can use the same techniques to carve smaller Santas that will hang nicely on a tree.

If you make the large ornament, you may want to display it on a stand rather than the tree. I've been experimenting with some stands. Some, you will see, were made by a blacksmith friend of mine, Johnny Kierbow, and are quite beautiful. The idea can probably be carried out by a smith in your area.

The other stands are made from wood, using power tools. The possibilities are endless, and it is fun to create the fanciful, even sensuous forms.

I hope you have fun with these. Judging by the demand I have found for them, they would make great gifts, and I am sure they will look great on your tree. Merry Christmas!

Carving the ornament

The blank for the ornament can be any thickness, from the width of pencil to 4 inches or more. It is important, though, that it be square.

Cut the line.

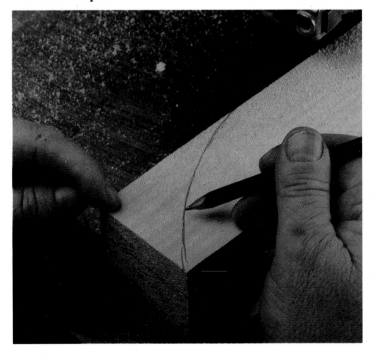

Cutting the basic curves on a bandsaw is most helpful. Begin by drawing a curve from about the middle of one side to the opposite corner.

Turn the blank 90 degrees, so the cut side is up, and draw the same line.

Cut that line. This brings one end of the blank to a point.

Rotate the blank 90 degrees and repeat. Draw...

Turn the piece end for end, keeping the same side against the saw table, and repeat the process. I want the points at each end to be on opposite corners, but you could choose a different corner to get a different effect. Draw the line...

and cut.

and cut it.

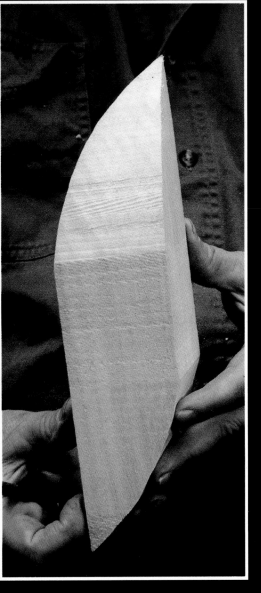

The result.

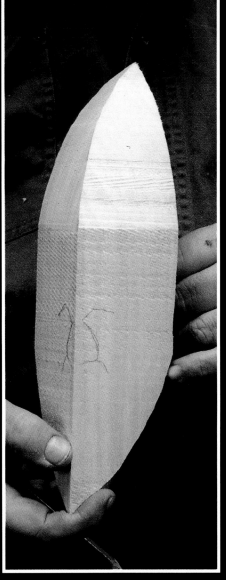

With this basic form your Santa design has a lot of options. With the nose here the cap goes back and the beard comes forward.

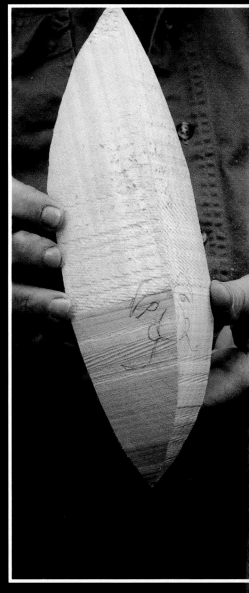

Here the hat comes forward and the beard back.

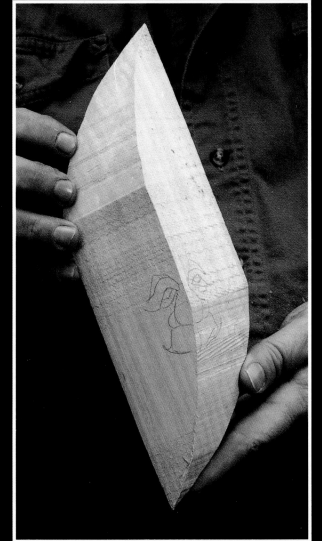

With the face on this corner, the hat and beard flow off to opposite sides. There are other options, and depending on where you place the face the Santa will take on a whole different character.

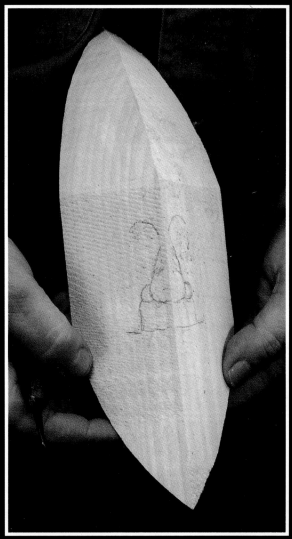

I've chosen to have the hat back and the beard forward. With Santas it is good to keep the nose wide and round and pudgy looking. A friendly Santa will have the moustache turned up, while a saintly Santa will have a Manchu-type moustache. I don't usually draw these, and after a little practice you probably won't either. The fact is that you really can't make a mistake on these Santas.

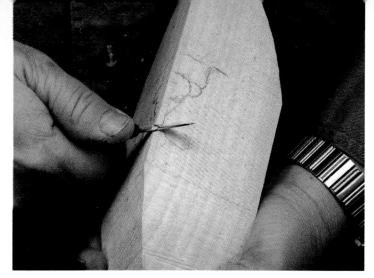

Cut a notch at the bridge of the nose, cutting at a 45 degree angle into the corner one way...

then the other.

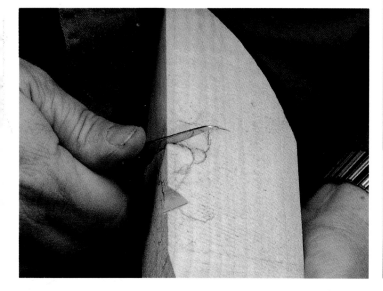

Make a straight stop at the bottom of the nose, rocking the knife to get deep.

Trim back to it from the moustache. The notch should be at least as deep as the bridge of the nose.

With these two cuts you can see a silhouette developing. All you should worry about now is bringing the nose out. The eyes and cheeks will naturally follow.

Keep the cuts nice and clean. Cut along the line of the nose, going into the wood at an angle.

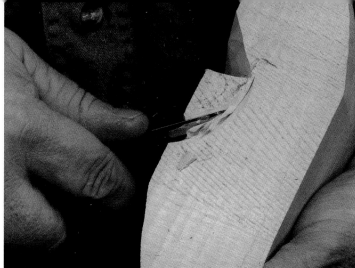

Repeat on the other side.

Slice back to clean up the cut.

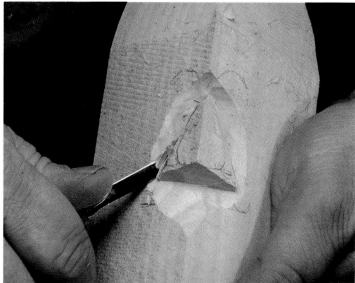

You are trying to create a surface plane all the way around the nose, bringing the nose out from the face.

Here you can see the result.

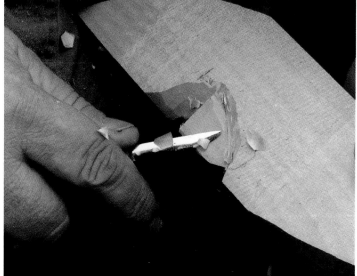

Clean up the lines, rounding off any ridges left by the knife.

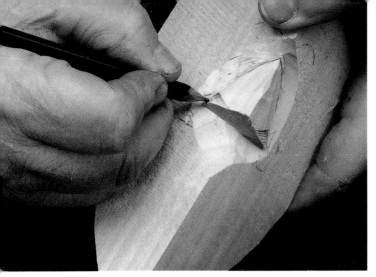

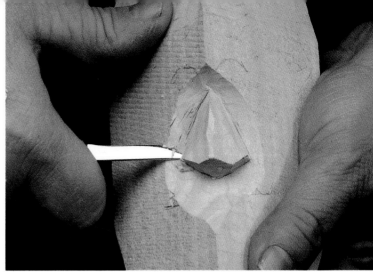

Knock off the back corners of the nose. This will begin the nostrils and shape the underside of the nose.

The result. Clean up the surface around the nose.

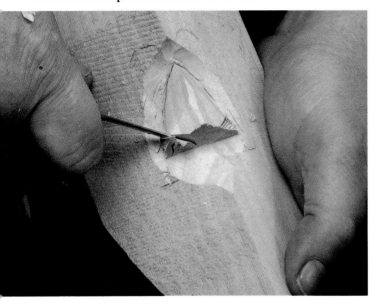

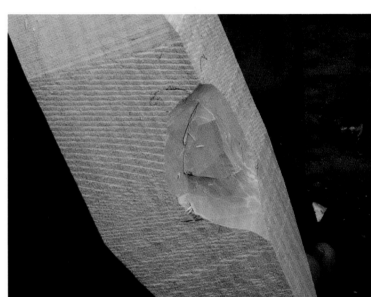

Cut straight into the corner...

The nose...

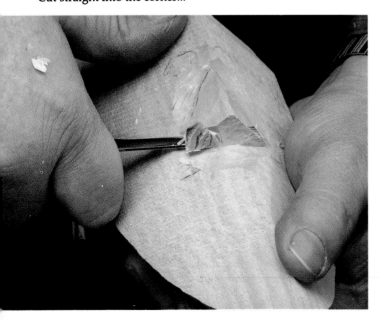

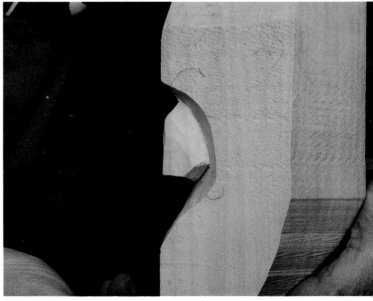

and nip it off from the moustache. Repeat on the other side.

is emerging pretty good.

The cheek line starts part way up the nose, slightly above the flare of the nostril. Make a stop line along the side of the nose about that high. Cut straight in.

The result. You don't want to bring the cheek line too far down the face until you are sure of the style and shape of the beard and moustache.

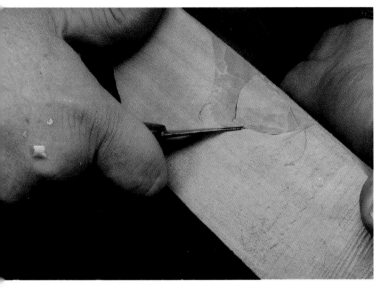

Come from the side of the nose down the cheek line with a cut angled 45 degrees down and 45 degrees in.

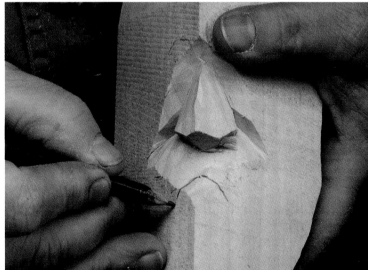

Draw the line of the lower edge of the moustache over the mouth.

Come back to the line with another cut, 45 degrees up and in.

Cut a stop straight in on one side...

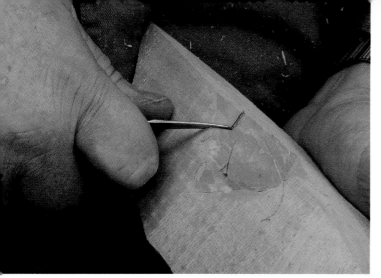

and the other.

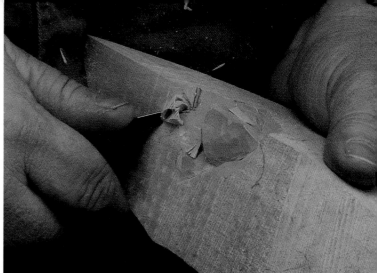

then deepen the cut.

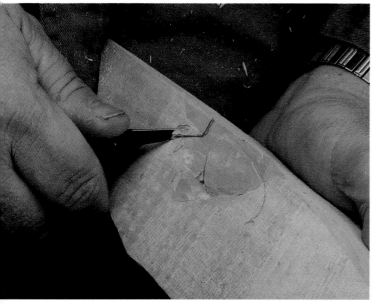

Cut back to the stops...

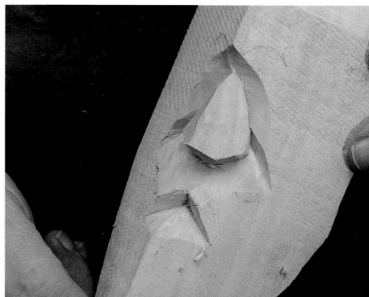

The result. We still don't want to go very far.

on both sides...

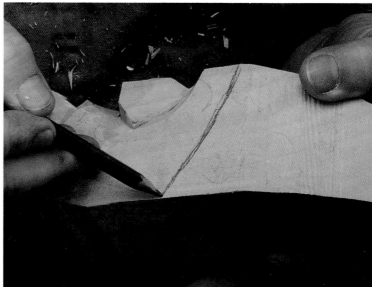

Establish the line of the hat. This fur lines goes above the forehead in the front, and travels down...

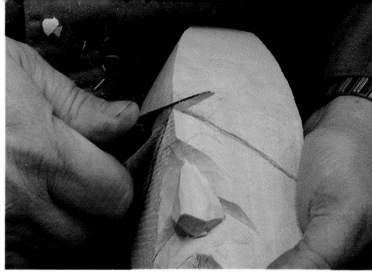

to a point in the back. Bring it up on the other side to join the point in the front.

At each corner of the hat cut a stop straight in...

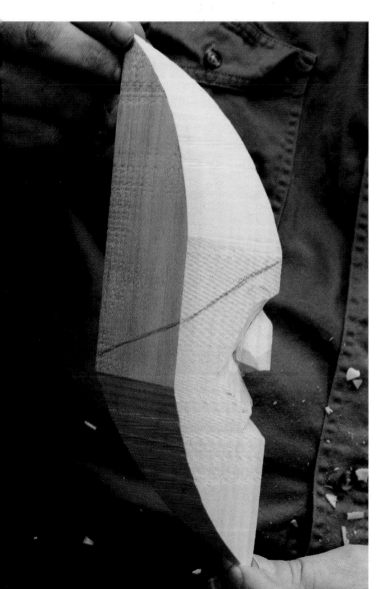

The line drawn.

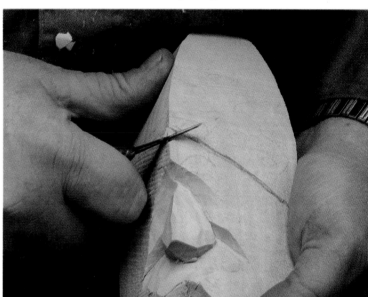

and trim back to it from the head.

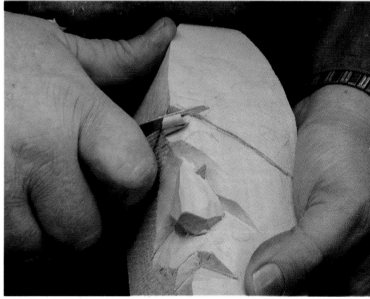

Repeat the process to deepen the cut.

 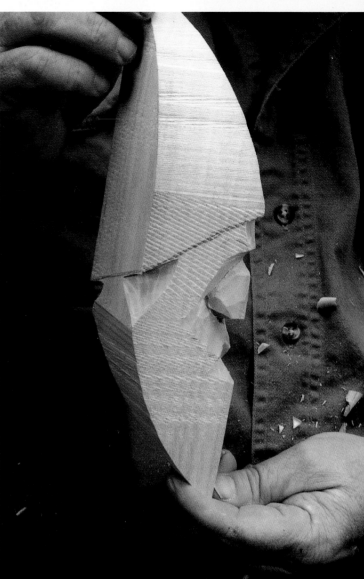

These views give you an idea of how deep to go.

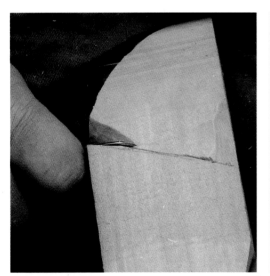  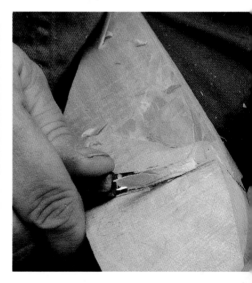

Working from corner to corner cut a stop along the hat line. You probably want to go over this 2 or 3 times to make it deep.

Trim back to it from the head.

Continue all around.

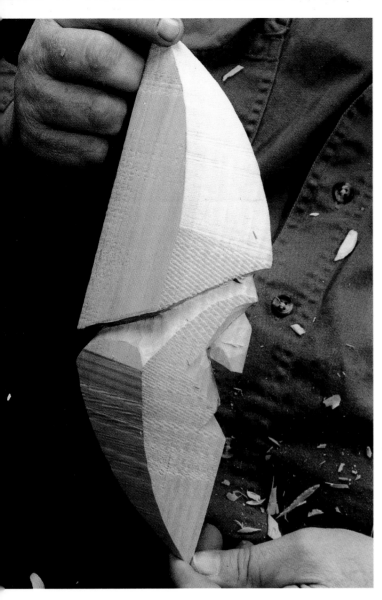

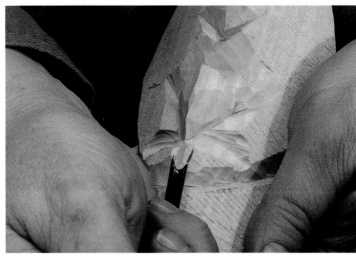

Separate the eyebrows by knocking out a nitch with the gouge.

This brings the hat out from the head.

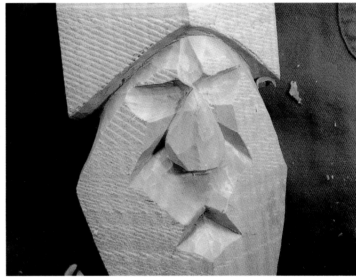

Progress. As you can see it is easy to create a mean looking Santa. It will take some work to make this guy look friendly.

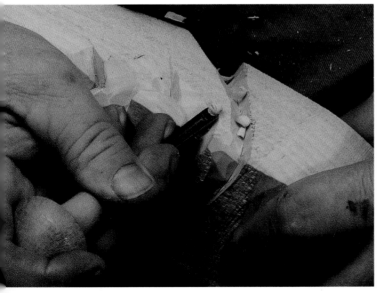

Working across the grain, use a palm gouge to create an eyesocket flowing out from the bridge of the nose.

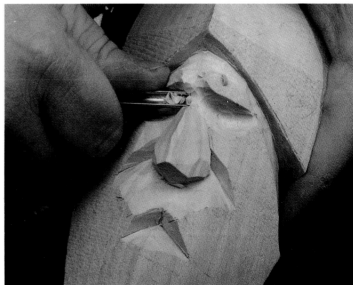

To do this I start by rounding out around the eyebrow and deepening the bridge of the nose.

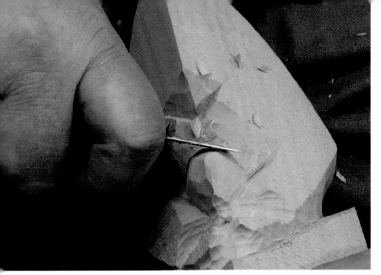

Begin shaping the nose by rounding off the sharp corners.

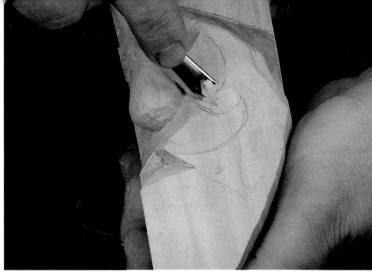

Come over the cheek with a gouge, keeping the cup against the work.

I am only taking off a little, so I can still decide on the shape. I am also working to make it symmetrical.

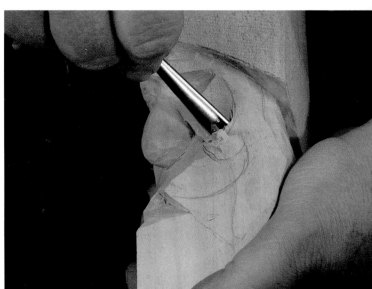

At the beard line push the gouge in to create a stop.

The softening features change the character.

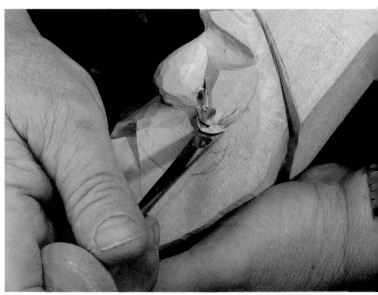

Come back to the cheek with the gouge, cup side up...

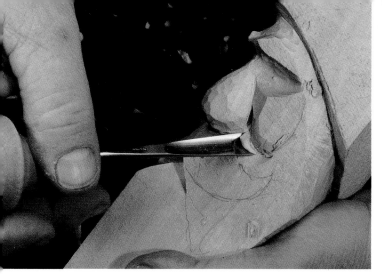

to trim it up.

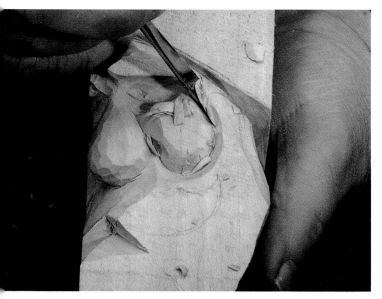

With the cup of the gouge away from the cheek, come over it and into the beard line at the temple.

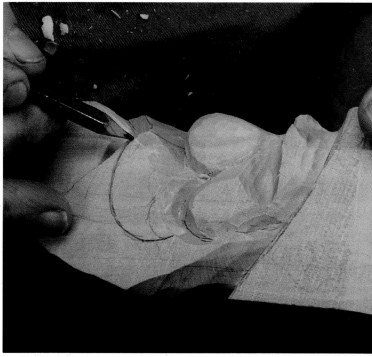

Repeat on the other side for this result.

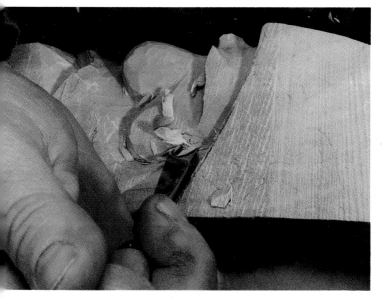

Chop it off.

Decide on the shape of the moustache and draw it in.

17

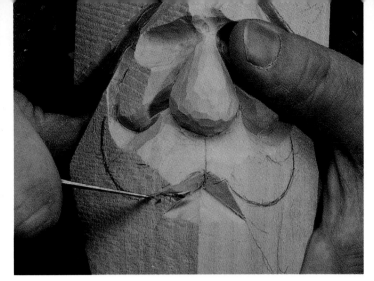

Cut a stop in the lower line of the moustache.

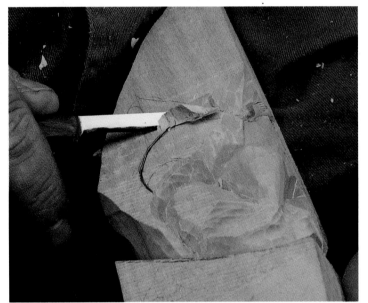

Cut back to it from the beard.

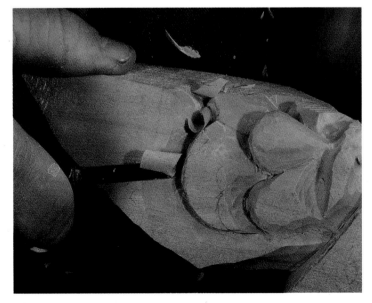

Flatten the angle of the beard.

Progress. He's getting more friendly with every cut!

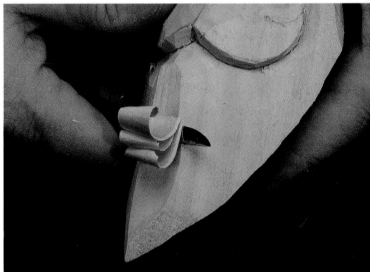

Trim off the front corner of the beard.

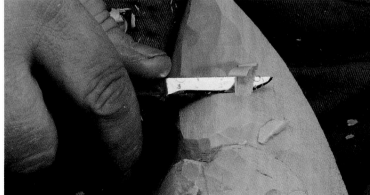

Shape the beard, leaving a place for an exaggerated bottom lip.

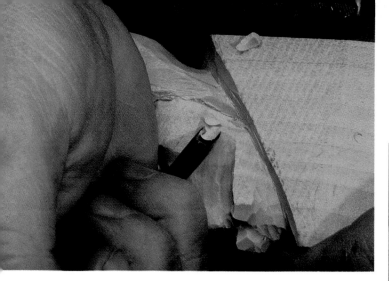

With a gouge continue the eyesockets into the temple.

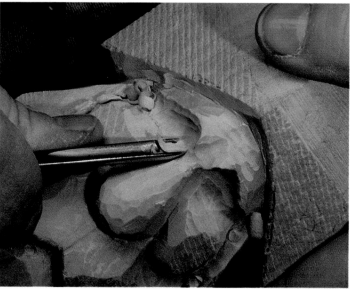

Deepen the eyesockets by coming up beside the nose with a gouge...

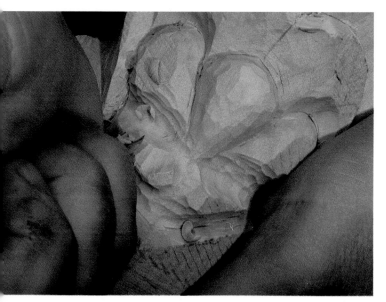

Give some lift to the eyebrow by going under it with a gouge. This gets rid of the frown.

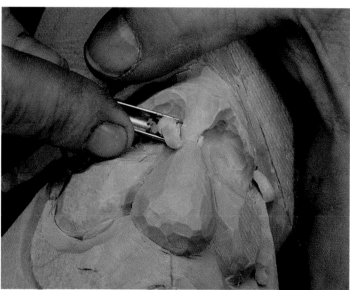

and coming back across the eyesocket to cut it off.

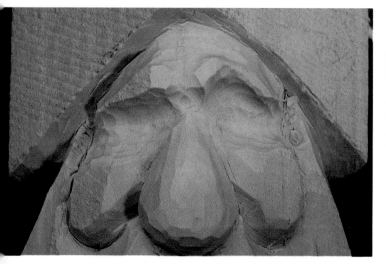

The eyebrow on the right is lifted. You can see how this will change the character of the face. I think I'll repeat it on the other side, although sometimes I might not want the eyebrows to be the same.

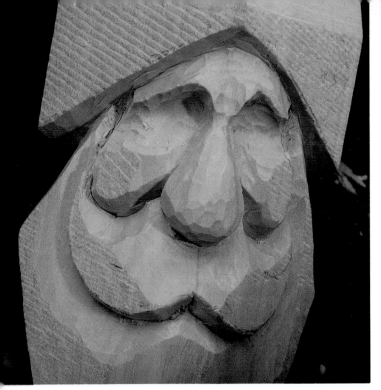

Progress. The mood is pretty well set now.

Establish the thickness of the fur of the hat.

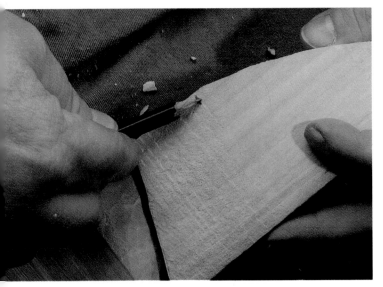

Use the finger and pencil to transfer the thickness to each corner.

Connect the marks.

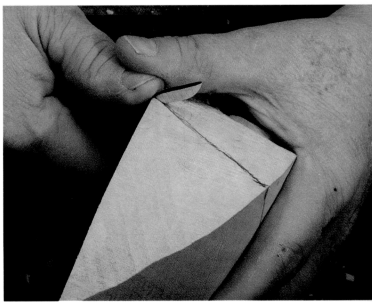

Cut a deep stop in the corner by rocking the knife.

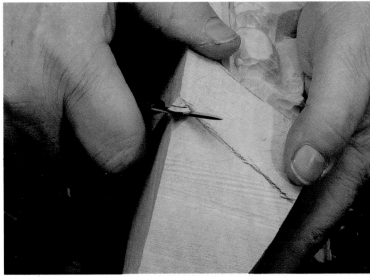

Come back to it from the hat.

20

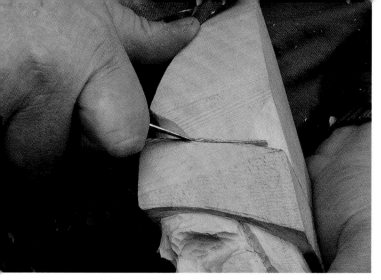

With the corners set, cut a stop along the line...

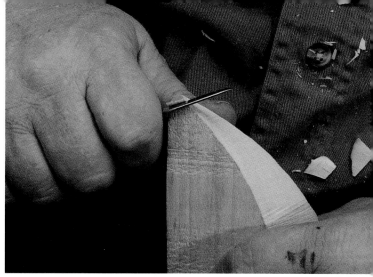

Begin to create the ball by nipping off the top.

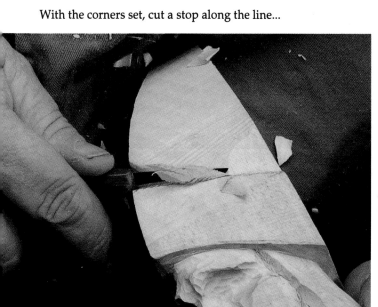

and cut back to it. Continue all around the hat.

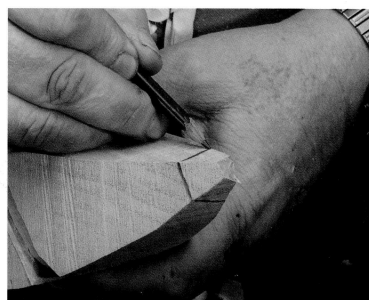

Define the area that will become the ball.

This should take you to about here.

Cut a stop in the corner...

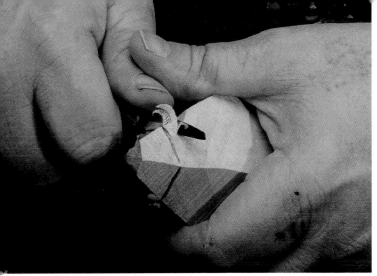

and come back to it from the hat. Repeat at the other corners.

This takes you to this point.

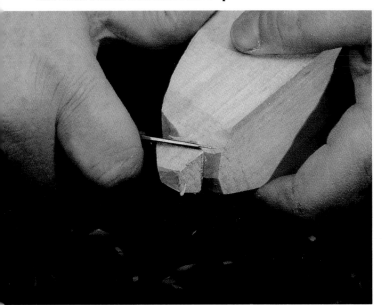

Cut a stop on the line between the corners...

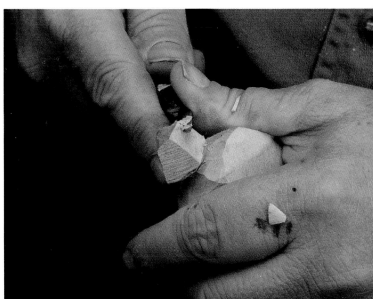

Knock the corners off the ball to take it to octagonal.

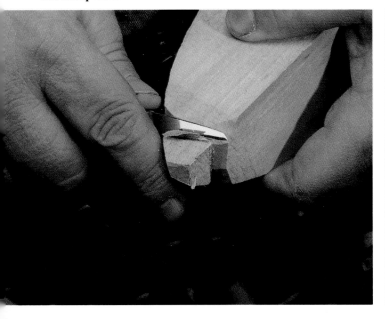

and trim back to it from the hat.

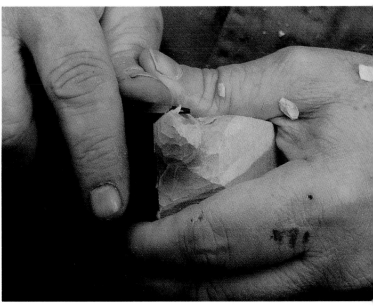

Round it into a ball.

The result.

Round up the crown of the hat.

Knock the corners off the hat.

Knock off the corners of the hat's trim, all the way around.

Take it to octagonal before rounding it. This step keeps things proportional and avoids the common problem of ending up with a flat looking figure.

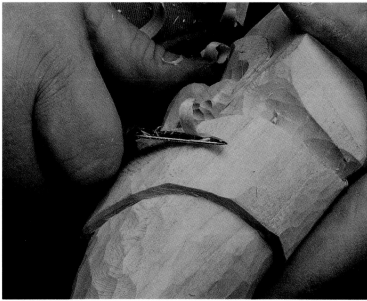

Go back and round up the trim.

Progress.

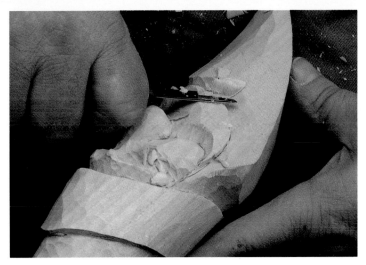

Go over the whole piece and clean up saw marks.

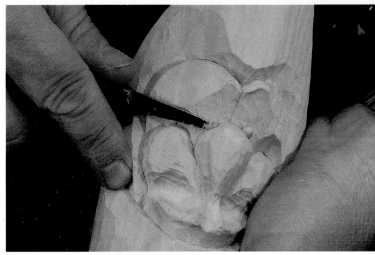

Cut off the wood with a knife.

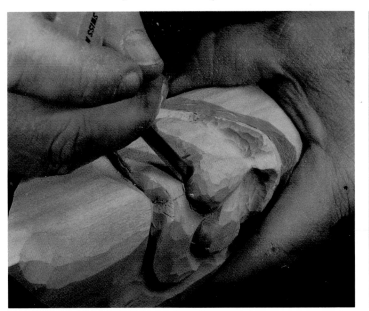

Create the nostril by coming straight into the underside of the nose with a half-round gouge.

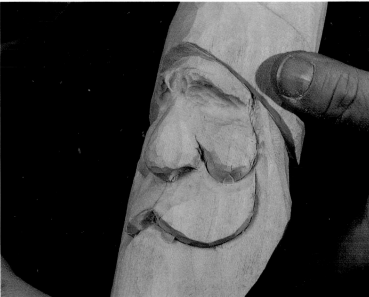

The result.

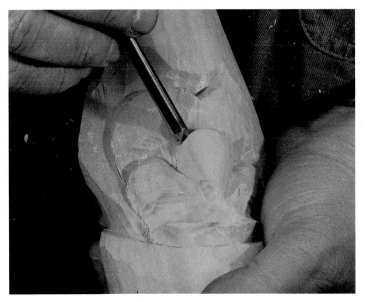

Do the same on the other side.

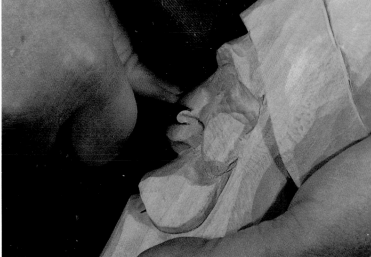

Come over the nostril with the same half-round, going up and over. Don't try to go deeper than your gouge or you'll bust up the surface.

The result.

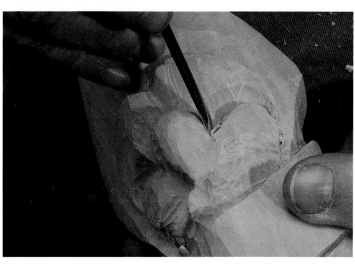

With the cup of the gouge against the nostril, smooth it out.

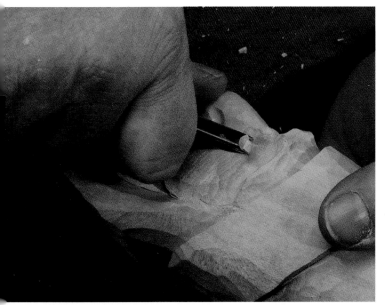

With the same gouge run up the side of the nose into the eye. This gives you a smooth transition into the cheek.

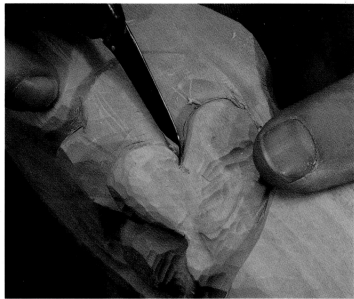

Clean out the corner where the nose and cheek meet with a knife. You want a nice, crisp line.

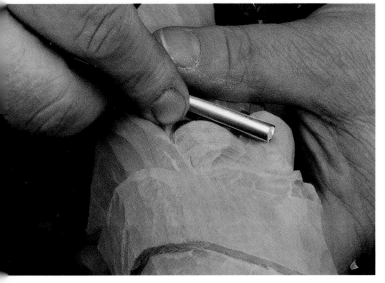

Blend the lines left by the half-round gouge with a flatter gouge.

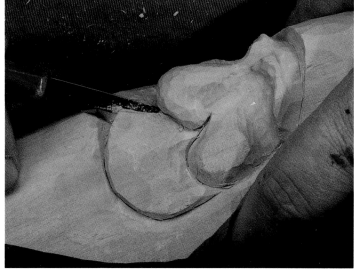

Create the separation in the moustache by coming down the middle with a knife, first on one side...

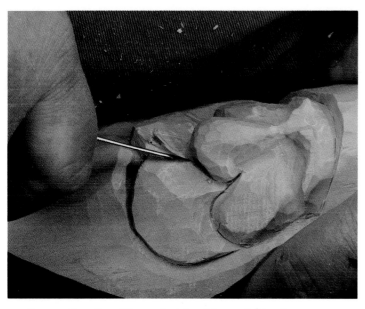

then on the other. The wedge should pop right out.

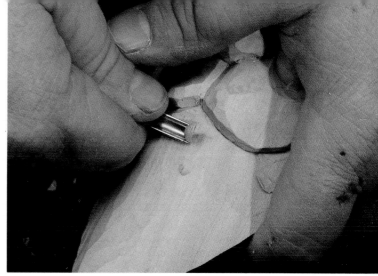

Bring out the bottom lip by gouging across the beard beneath it.

Progress on the face.

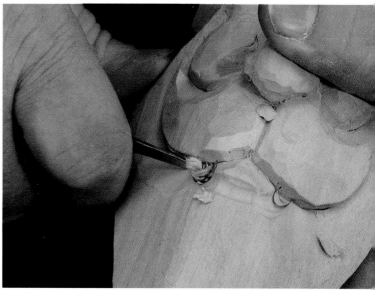

Clean up the corners with a knife.

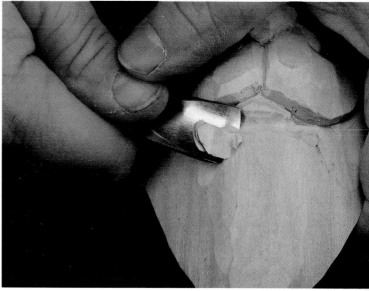

Use a wider gouge to smooth the transition into the beard below the mouth.

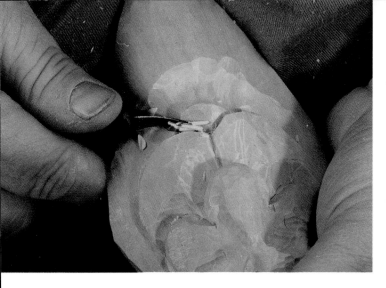

Use a knife to shape the lower lip.

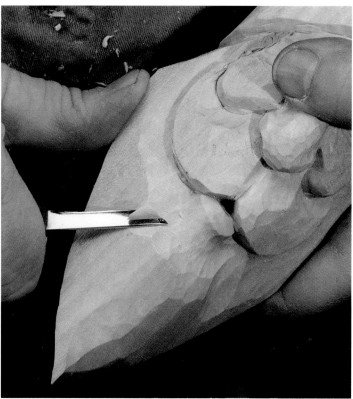

Shape the beard at the lower corners of the mouth. This gives the look of the chin shaped under the beard.

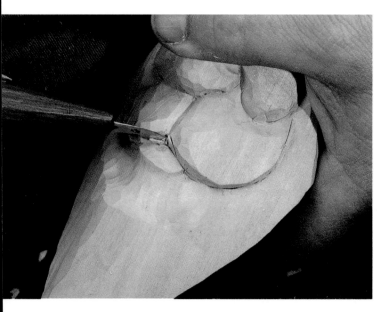

The point of the knife will open the mouth just a little. What you are really doing is putting the shadow back in there.

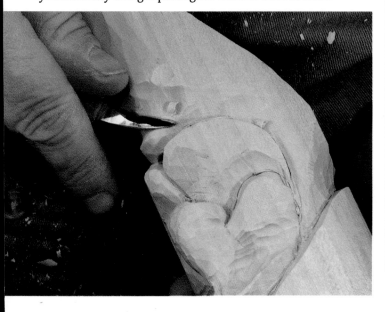

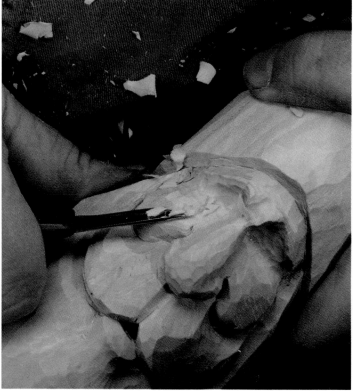

Go over and refine the cheek and other areas of the face.

Smooth the underside of the lip with a knife.

Progress.

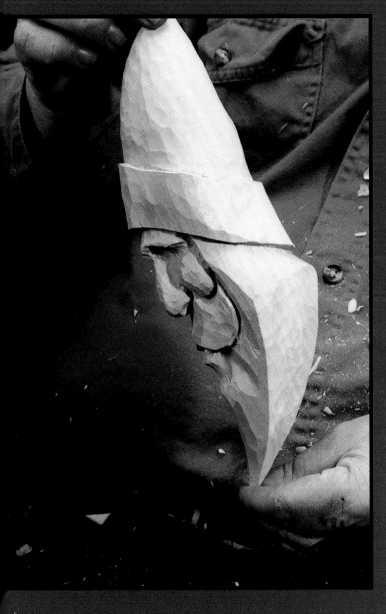

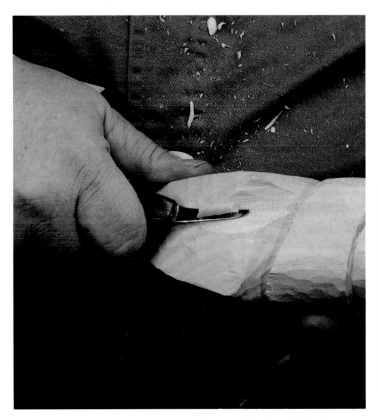

A groove running down the back side of the beard help bring it out.

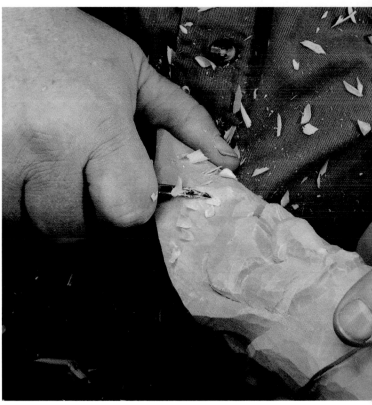

Go over the face to smooth the big, bold cuts.

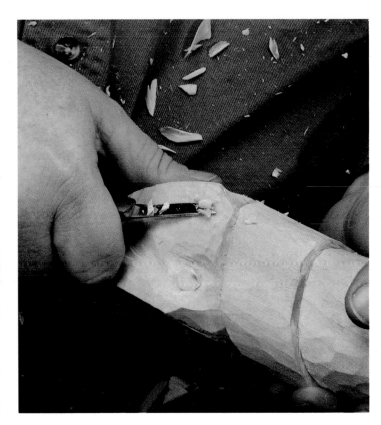

Shape below the trim in the back. I'm going to leave the main ridge in place.

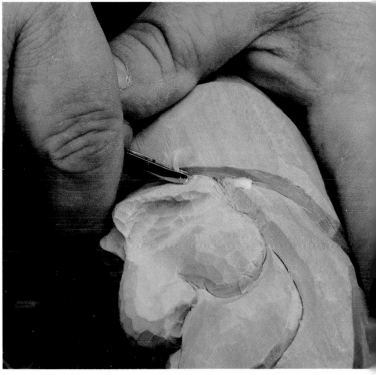

Run a veiner around the outline of the eyebrows to bring them out. I've just about decided not to put hair lines in this Santa, so the eyebrows need some shadow to bring them to life.

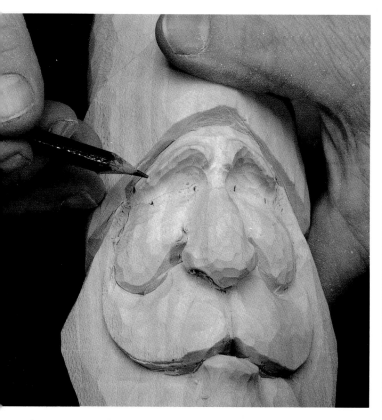

Establish the placement of the eyes. Imagine five eyes end-to-end across the face. The second and the fourth are going to be the ones we use for the eyes.

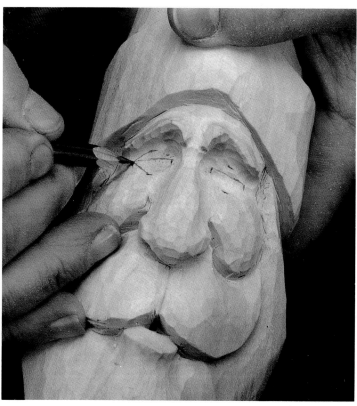

A dot above and below the middle of the eye will give the line for its top and bottom curves.

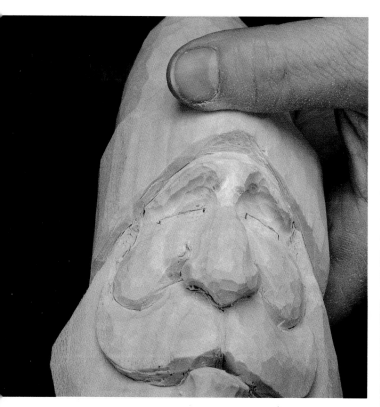

Draw a line from side to side across the eyes. This is a reference for the angle of the eyes. If it doesn't look right, draw it again!

With the eyes drawn add the lids, top and bottom.

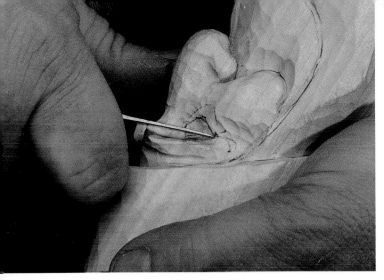

At each corner of the eye you need to make three cuts. First cut straight in along the upper lid.

The outside corners done.

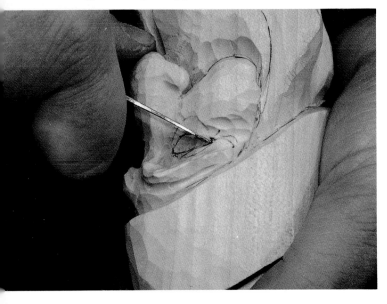

Then cut along the lower lid.

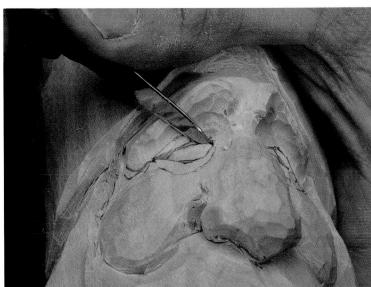

Repeat on the...

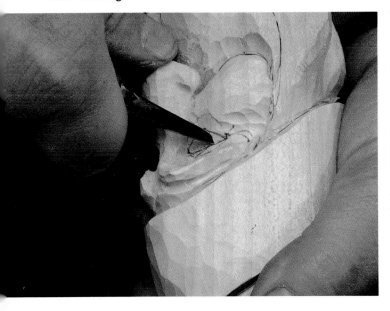

Then, with your blade flat against the eyeball, slice into to the corner to pop out a triangle. Repeat at each corner.

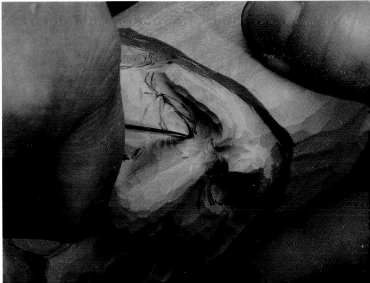

inside...

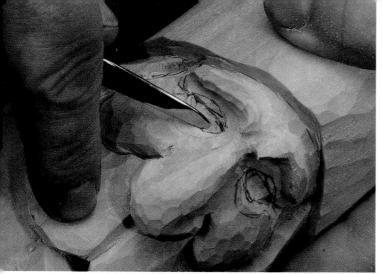

corners.

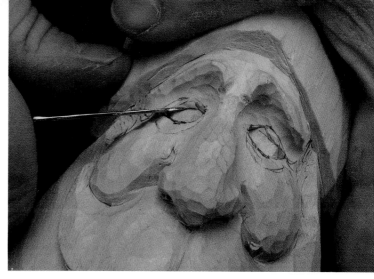

Cut back to the stop from the eyeball to round off the eye.

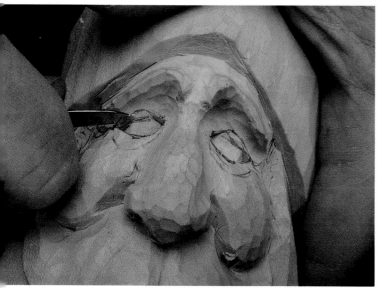

Cut a stop on the line of the eyelid, above...

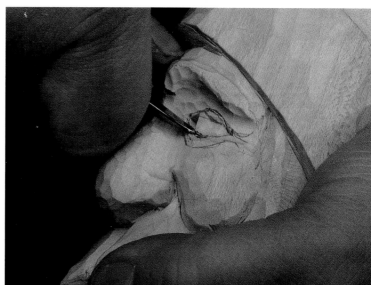

Repeat on the other eye.

and below.

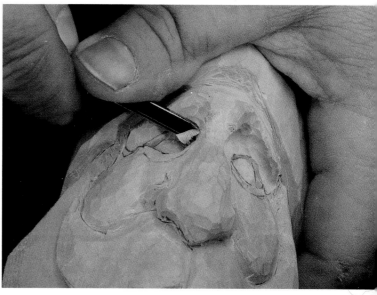

Use a veiner to create a lid above the eye. This is a little higher than the line we drew.

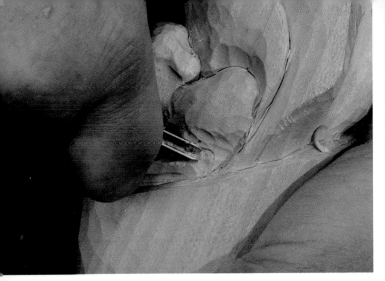

Carry the line around and into the temple.

Progress on the eyes.

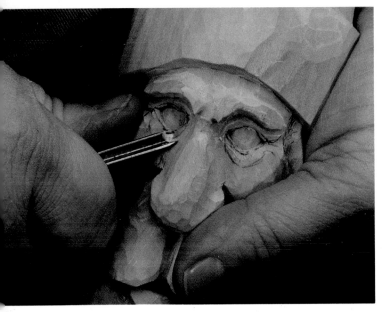

Do the same to create the lower lid.

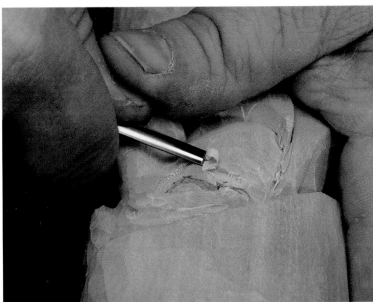

Use a wider gouge to soften the lines of the lids.

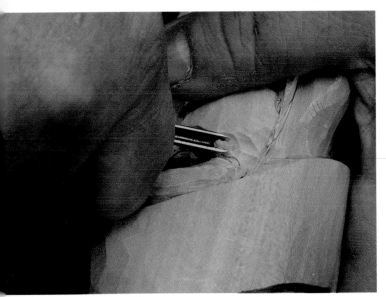

Again, carry the line around to the temple.

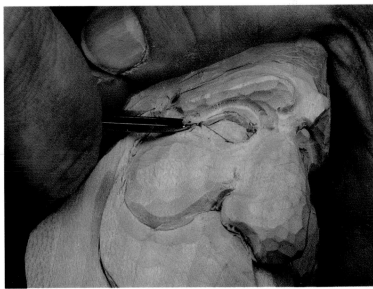

With a small veiner add some crow's feet to the corners of the eyes.

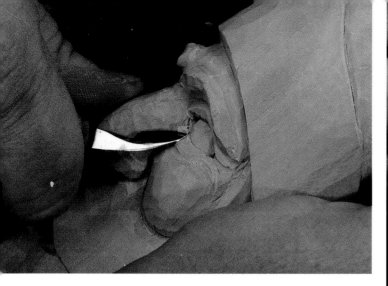

A knife will clean things up and erase the pencil marks. Any time you work near the eyes it is helpful to have some magnification.

Go over the whole carving, cleaning it up with a knife.

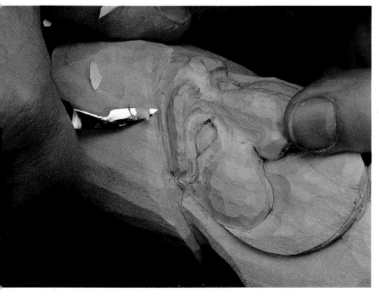

Soften the line of the hat trim.

Ready to paint.

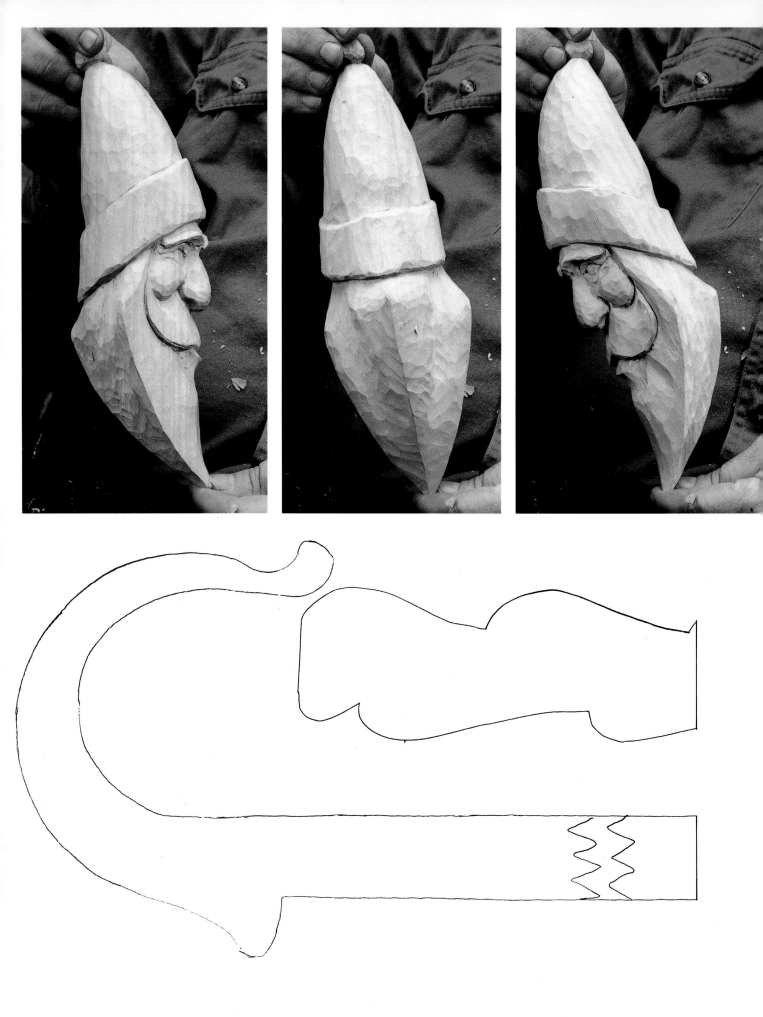

the stand

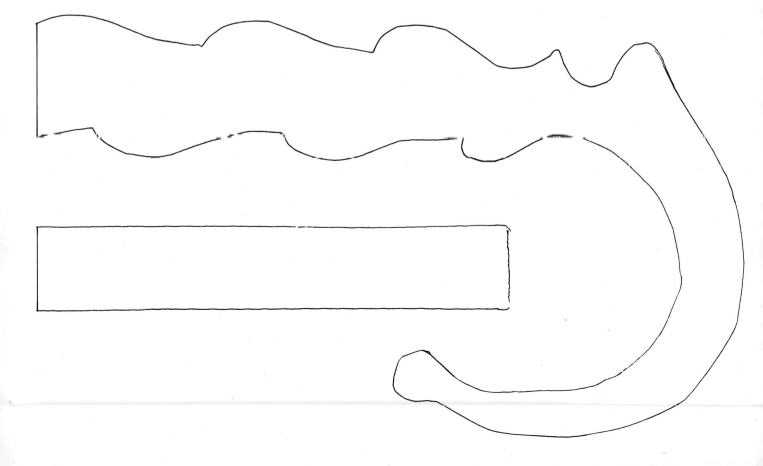

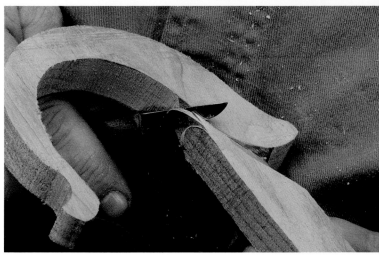

Cut the pattern for the stand from 5" board of 3/4" thick wood. I used butternut. The length will depend on the height of the ornament you are going to hang on it. Draw the detail of the top.

Do the same on the inside corners.

Cut a stop into the corner...

When the corners are done, cut a stop along the rest of the line...

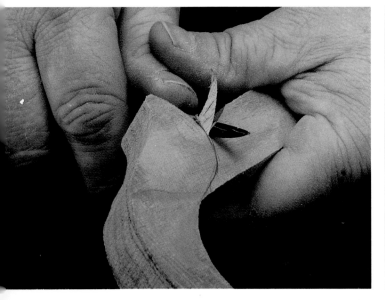

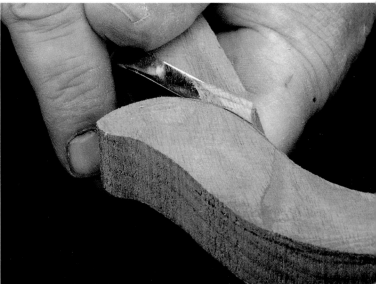

and trim back to it from the shaft.

and trim back to it.

40

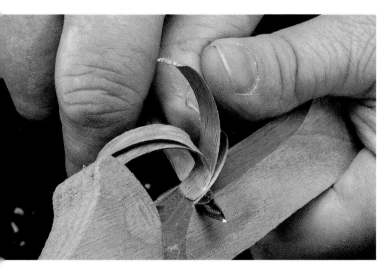

Shave the corners off the shaft to take it to octagonal.

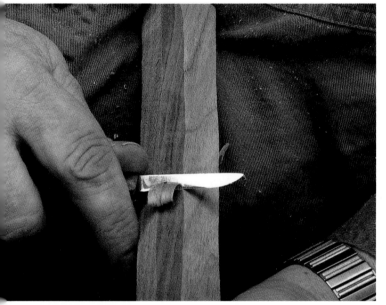

Don't go all the way to the end for now.

Repeat on the other edges. The direction of your cut will depend on the direction of the grain.

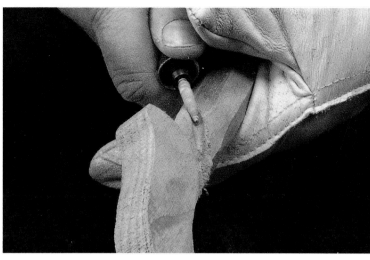

Using a Cutz-all bit we will create the spiral in the shaft. You can draw the line to follow, but I find that just holding the tool at one angle and turning the shaft works well. Notice the glove. This bit will chew up your hand.

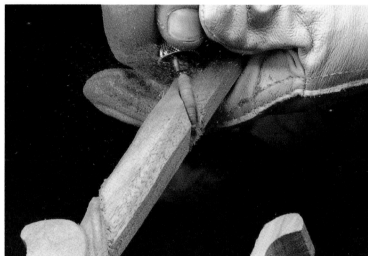

Work your way down the shaft.

Try to achieve the same depth with each cut.

The first spiral done.

Start opposite the beginning of the first spiral and create a second.

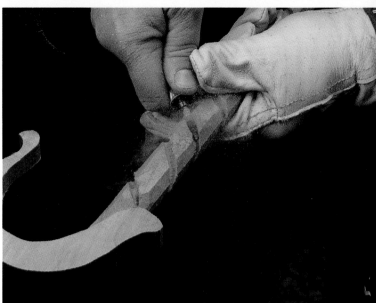

This will run right between the first.

The result.

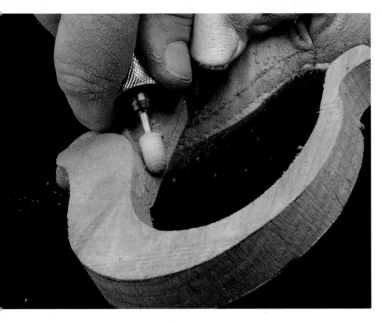

Change to a bigger burr to widen the spiral grooves.

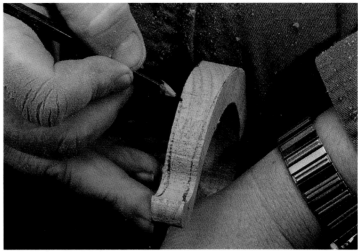

Draw the width of the hook.

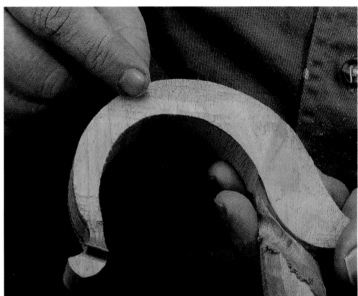

This top part of the hook is cross grain so it will break if you're not careful. Since it isn't holding much weight, it will be fine for our ornament stand.

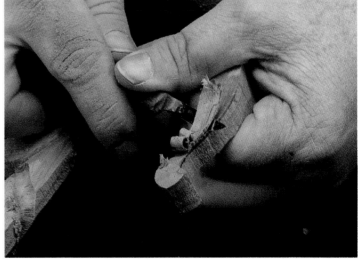

Trim the sides of the hook.

Progress.

Knock the corners off the back end of the hook.

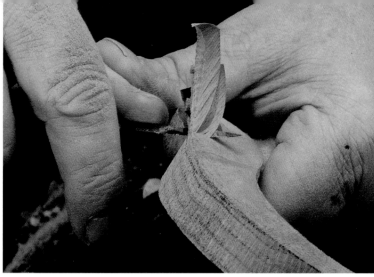

Knock off the top edges of the hook, in preparation for rounding. The bottom surface will stay squarer for added strength.

Round over the under side of the knob.

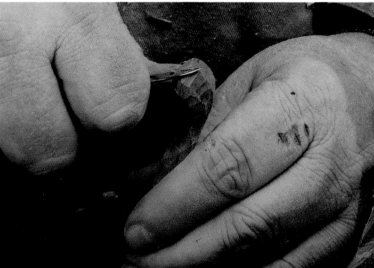

You want the front knob of the hook to relate to the back knob, so try to make it about the same. Begin by rounding the underside.

Progress.

The result.

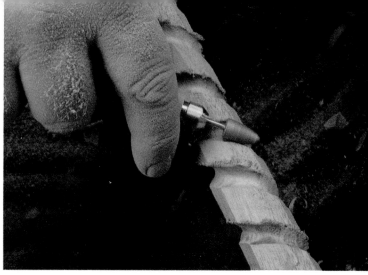

Don't forget to do both spiral grooves.

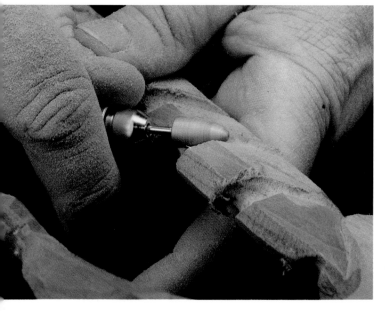

With a ruby bit I take out the rough marks left in the spiral grooves by the previous bit.

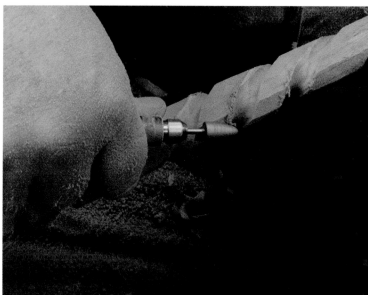

Use the same bit to knock the fuzzies off the edges of the grooves.

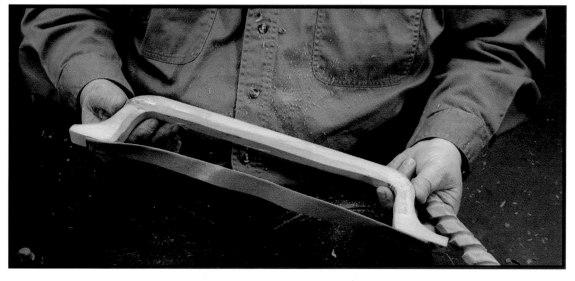

This fiddle bow sander is easy to make and makes easy work of sanding the shaft of this hook.

Go over the whole surface of the shaft, knocking off the rough edges.

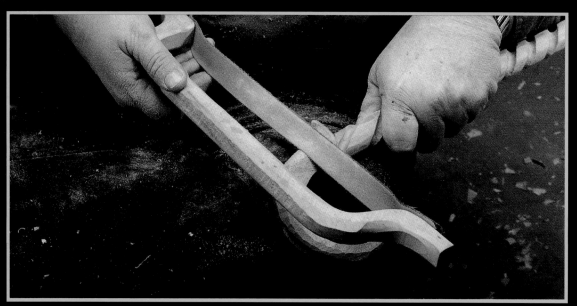

Continue on the handle.

By going across the grain the fiddlebow sander leaves a lot of little scratches. This final hand sanding takes them out.

The application of a stain brings the grain alive. For this piece I'm using Briwax™, a staining wax.

Cut the base from a six inch board. It is cut octagonal on the table saw and molded with a router.

I apply the wax with a piece of steel wool. This helps take away any fuzzies left in the wood. Smear it on real good.

While the base dries apply the wax to the hook.

Do the same with the hook.

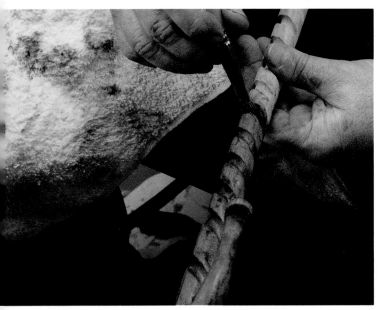

You may need a brush to get it down in the spiral grooves.

When it is completely dry, polish it to a nice soft shine. If the finish is too heavy when it dries, you can lighten it with turpentine.

The finish dries quickly and can be polished with a cloth. After it sits for a few minutes wipe away the excess and put the piece aside to dry. (Because it dries quickly you need to keep the can of the Briwax closed when not in use.)

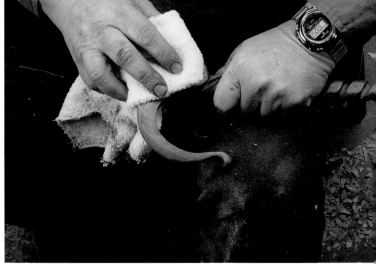

Repeat on the shaft.

An eyelet opened up with needle-nosed pliers goes into the hook. The ornament will hang from this.

Counter sink a hole in the bottom of the stand.

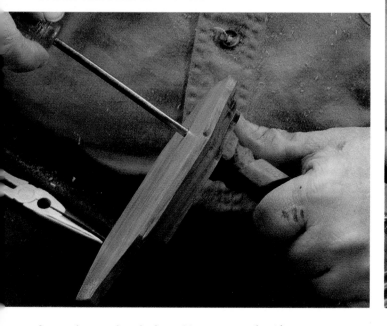

Screw the stand to the base. You can use glue if you want to.

The result.

painting santa

For wood carving I use Winsor and Newton Alkyd tube paints. Most coats are thinned with pure turpentine to a consistency that is soaked into the carving, giving subtle colors. What I look for is a watery mixture, almost like a wash. In this way the turpentine will carry the pigment into the wood, giving the stained look I like. It has always been my theory that if you are going to cover the wood, why use wood in the first place. It should be noted that with white, the concentration of the pigment should be a little stronger.

I mix my paints in juice bottles, putting in a bit of paint and adding turpentine. I don't use exact measurements. Instead I use trial and error, adding a bit of paint or a bit of turpentine until I get the thickness I want.

The juice bottles are handy for holding your paints. They are reclosable, easy to shake, and have the added advantage of leaving a concentrated amount of color on the inside of the lid and the sides of the bottle which can be used when more intense color is needed.

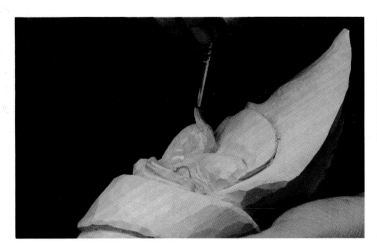

Paint the skin with a mixture of raw sienna, white, and a touch of tube flesh or pink.

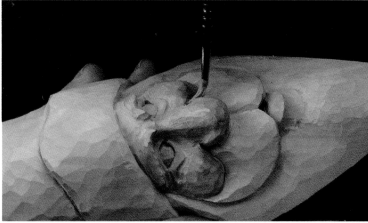

Add red to the forehead, nose, lip, and cheeks.

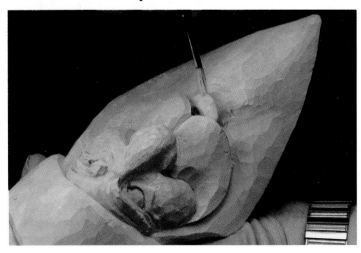

Don't forget the lip and below.

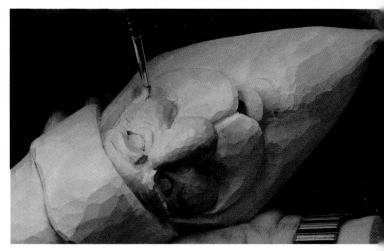

Work it into flesh.

Apply white to the beard...

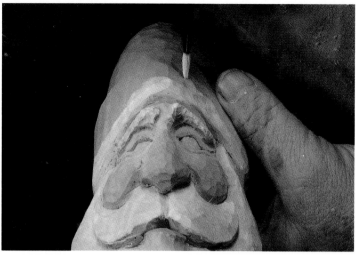

and the trim. Start at the edge with a smaller brush...

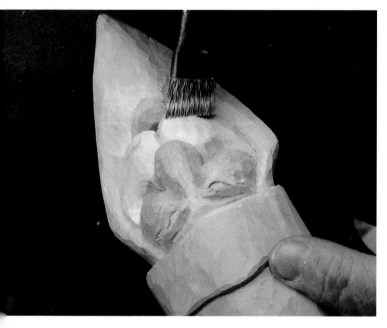

the moustache...

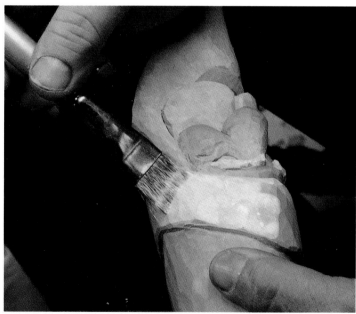

and a wider brush to do the flat surface.

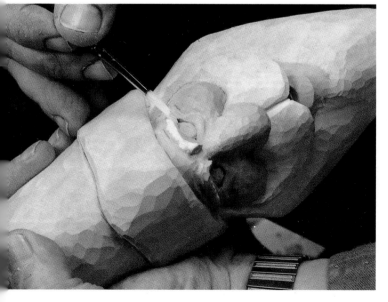

the eyebrows...

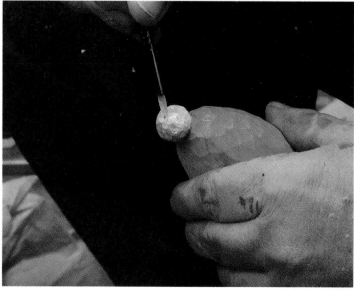

Don't forget the ball.

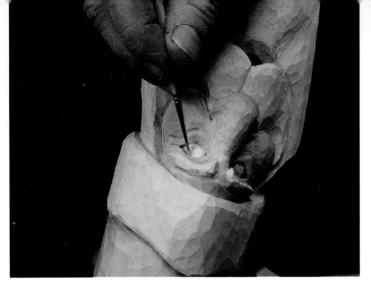

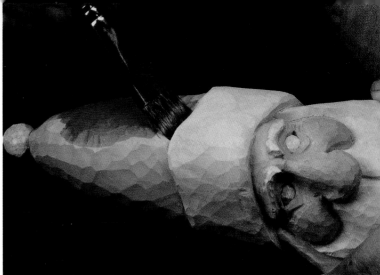

Apply a heavier white pigment to the eyeball. I usually get this from the inside of the cap of my white paint jar.

The red is an Alizarin crimson wash.

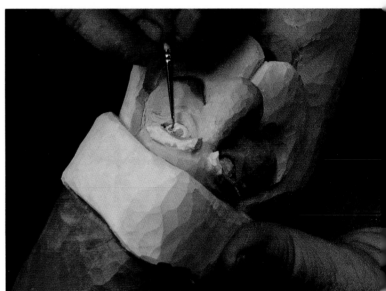

The eyes are light blue and looking slightly up.

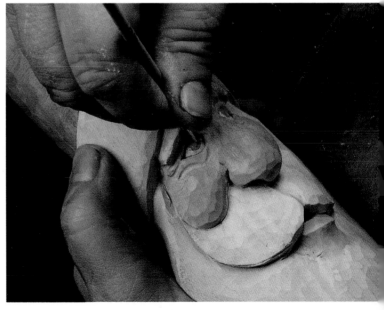

The white finished.

Do the other eye the same way.

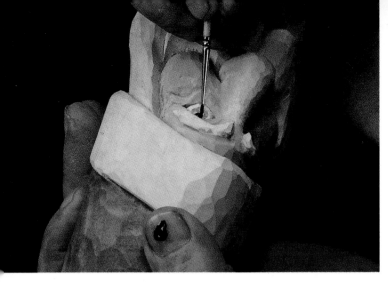

The pupil is black and uses the heavy pigment from the paint bottle cap. My thumb is my palette.

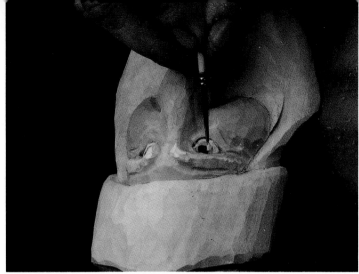

The white speck should be in the same position in each eye.

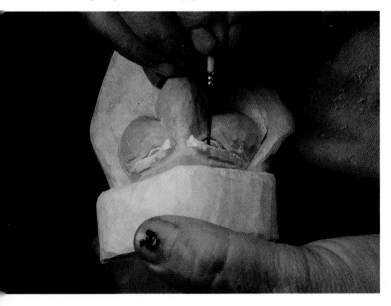

Do the other eye to match.

The eyes finished.

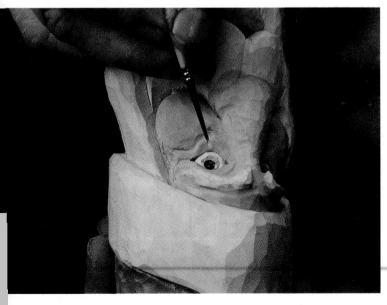

A white glint in the eye should finish it off. Use thick pigment again.

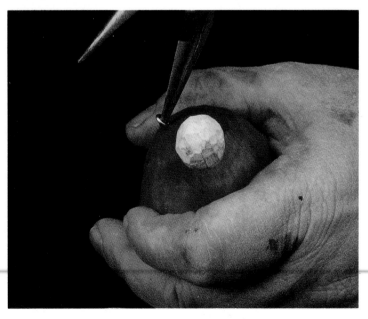

Put an eye hook in the cap.

Finis!!!

the santa gallery

58

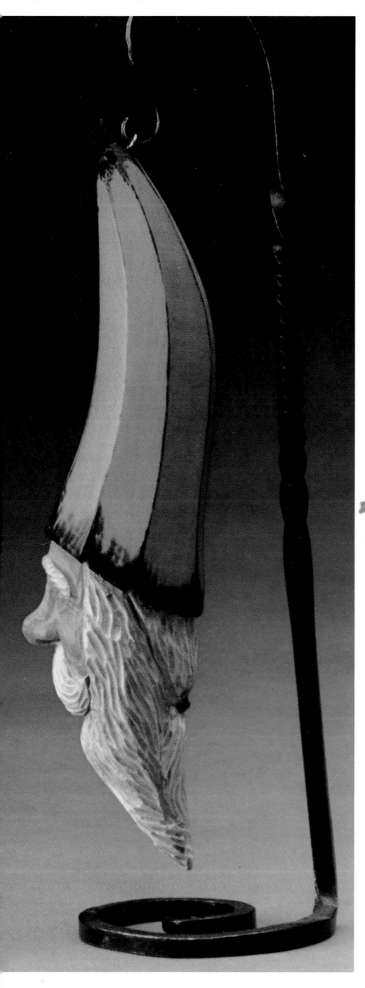